Living

With

Ghosts

Understanding and Managing Paranormal Activity Within Your Home

*THIS BOOK IS DEDICATED TO MY
FAMILY AND TO ALL OF THE
SPIRITS, WHO HAVE AMAZED ME
THROUGHOUT THE YEARS.*

A LETTER TO MY READERS

Dear Friend,

I am not a trained Para-Psychologist. Nor, am I a highly paid professional in the paranormal field. I am just a normal person who has lived with paranormal activity all of my life. I am a sensitive. Also known as, a physical medium. I have the gift of seeing, hearing, and feeling spirits.

After moving into a haunted house in 2000, I did extensive research about paranormal activity. With over forty years of having unexplained events happen randomly in my life, I too, learned new facts and techniques that I never knew existed.

I wanted to write this book so other people who deal with paranormal activity in their lives, could comprehend what they are witnessing, learn how calm and reclaim their homes, and feel more confident about themselves when dealing with the bizarre and unknown world of the paranormal.

I have tried to do this in an easy to follow guide. After reading this book I hope you have a better understanding of the activity in your home, how to manage it, and progress to a favorable outcome for you and the spirits in your home.

Sincerely,

Rebecca June Williford

MY EXPERIENCE WITH THE PARANORMAL

Ever since I was a young child I have always had experiences with paranormal activity. Back then, it wasn't something everybody was talking about. In fact it was basically a forbidden subject. People thought you were crazy or losing your mind! So, I usually kept everything I ever witnessed to myself.

The earliest memory I have of paranormal activity was seeing little lights in my room at night. They would flit around like little fairies. I was never scared of them. I also really didn't know what they were either. I can remember being very uneasy about going down to my father's workshop in the first house I lived in. Something about that room just never felt right. I always felt like a large man was watching me when I was in there.

When I was going to school I hated going on historical field trips. I had a really hard time going anywhere near a historical building, cemeteries, or battlefields. I almost felt smothered with all the energies surrounding me. It terrified me! I tried to avoid sacred grounds at all costs.

When I was about eight years old, I had my first dream that I found out later would come true. I dreamed that a family was out on a small boat and their little dog drowned. The following day a little girl, who went to my church, came over to my house. She told me that her family was planning a boating trip on the river on Saturday. My stomach dropped. I looked her dead in the eyes and said "Don't take your dog with you!" She asked why and I couldn't answer her. Of course, she looked at me like I had three heads and walked away.

That Sunday during church, it was announced that the family had a tragic boating accident. The small boat had capsized. Everyone aboard was ok, except their little puppy who had drowned! I was shocked! I actually had to get up and go to the bathroom and get sick. I never told anyone that I knew that boating accident would happen before it did. I hoped I would never have a dream like that ever again.

When I was a teenager, I started seeing full body apparitions. We had a ghost in our house that I could see out of the corner of my eye while I was watching TV. As soon as I would turn to look at it, the solid white figure would run down the hall and fade into the back wall. One night my brother and I were watching a movie together. All of a sudden I heard him say, "Did you just see that?" I said, "What the white ghost running down the hall?" He was surprised when I said that without even looking up. Again, we kept this information to ourselves.

This was also the time in my life I had another life altering dream. It was a early fall night. Thursday, to be exact. I dreamed that a girl I went to High School with was in a horrible car accident. I saw it happen in my dream! This time I knew who it was going to happen to and when it would occur! I saw her getting into a car after a Friday night football game. I saw her sitting in the middle of the front seats on the console. After a short drive in the country, they went around a corner on a back road too fast and crashed into a tree. She went flying through the windshield cutting her face along the right cheek. Everyone else in the car escaped serious injury and walked away.

The following day at school I walked up to this girl and said, "I know we are not friends and I know what I am about to say is going to sound really strange. But, after the game tonight Please don't sit on the console if you go out in a car!" She asked why and I told her that I had a dream about her last night and to please listen to what I had told her. She just looked at me like I was crazy and walked off whispering and giggling with her cheerleader friends, letting them know what a freak I was. Oh well, at least I had tried to warn her! I went on with my day. Who cares what they thought!

The next Monday rolled around. As I was putting my books in my locker the halls were abuzz with news of a bad car accident that happened on Friday night! Later that day I found out that it had happened just the way I had dreamed it would! The pretty girl had to have plastic surgery to repair the cut on her right cheek. When she finally came back to school she never looked at me the same way again. I think it really spooked her. I never told anyone about this and I don't think she ever did either.

When I was in my early twenties is when I started having some of my most extreme experiences. A friend of mine had bought an old farm house on the outskirts of Richmond, Virginia. It had once been used as a civil war field hospital. The floors still had blood stains on them and in the master bedroom you could tell where the operating table once stood in front of the fireplace. I was a divorced single Mom at the time and my friend and her family had always been so good to us by including us in their lives.

One night my daughter and I were invited to stay the night at the farm house. I was trying to fall asleep in the living room on the sofa, like I had done so many times before. Everyone else in the house was asleep. I turned over to face the back of the sofa I pulled the knitted blanket up to my waist and started to doze off. Suddenly, I felt someone tucking the blanket gently around my legs all the way up to my waist. I turned over to see who was doing this and there wasn't anyone there! I freaked out! I felt a scream caught in my chest that would not come out do to my terror! I went to the bathroom and splashed some cold water on my face and finally went back to the sofa. I left the blanket on the floor the rest of the night! I never told anybody about this either. I don't think they would have believed me anyway.

About a year later, at the same house, my friends and I were enjoying a wonderful glass of wine in the master bed room. Out of the corner of my eye I noticed a bright light coming through the hinge side of the door. I figured the kids were playing with a flashlight in the living room so, I didn't think much more about it.

About a minute later I saw an orb the size of a basketball come through the door. It was floating slowly between us about three feet off the floor. I had to speak up! I asked if anyone else was seeing this. My friend's husband said he did and it was changing colors. He was right it was changing colors! It went from bright white to pink to light blue to a pale green before it vanished! I was so happy that someone else saw what I did! Finally I didn't feel so different! My friend denied seeing it. I don't know the reason. I guess she was afraid to admit it.

When I was 30, I remarried and had my second child. We moved to a old farmhouse that sat on the fringe of Saylors Creek Battlefield in Rice, Virginia. I never saw anything in the house but, there was a back room I never liked to be in by myself. It had a strange vibe to it.

After my son was about six weeks old, I finally got to go back to work as a bartender. My job was in Farmville, Virginia, which was a good forty five minute drive from our home. The only problem I had with the drive was, I had to go through the battlefield by myself in the wee hours of the morning.

Every night after closing down the bar, I would climb in our SUV and happily cruise down the back roads towards home. When I approached the battlefield road I would turn the radio down low and slowly make the left turn onto the dark road. Slowly make my way across the bridge. Then up the hill that was in the center of the large empty field. Most of the time, it was eerie, but uneventful. Until, one night, when I was crossing the bridge.

A little ways up the road, I saw a man in a gray suit walking along the right shoulder. As I approached him, I could see him clearly in my headlights. But, when I got right up to him he wasn't there. I stopped the Blazer and looked into the darkness on both sides of the field. He had vanished into thin air!

A few weeks later I was topping the hill, and to my right I saw a figure of a man on a white horse. He was looking over the battlefield holding a flag. When I took a double take the figure had disappeared. I always respected the fallen solders by driving slowly and turning my music down. I don't know why they decided to let me see them, but I am very thankful they did.

I did tell my husband and daughter what I saw while driving home. My daughter believed me. I'm still not sure my husband ever did. After I told them, there was this running question about what I saw on the drive home the night before. Most of the time, it was a disappointment. Other times I would tell them I saw the man walking beside the road again. I got to the point the late night drive didn't bother me at all. It was more like a ghostly adventure.

Later that year, my new family and I moved to the mountains of East Tennessee. Our house is an old stone house that was built in 1948. Little did we know what awaited use behind the old antique doors.

The first full day I was in the house, I started having paranormal experiences. Throughout the years we have all heard voices, seen full body apparitions, and I have even had a spirit touch me. I won't give everything away in this book. So if you want to know the whole story you will have to read my first book,

Ghosts of the Old Stone House:

Personal Accounts of a Haunting in East Tennessee.

It is on sale now in online bookstores.

I hope this information proves to you that I really do know what I am talking about when it comes to the paranormal. Over the years I have done extensive research on this subject and with my personal experience I hope to help you understand how to live peacefully with the ghosts that wander between this world and the other side.

IS MY HOUSE REALLY HAUNTED?

This is my check list, and how I determine if a house is really haunted.

1. Is there a history of paranormal activity?

2. Has a tragic event happened in the house or on the property it stands on?

3. Has there been death in the house or on the surrounding property?

4. Is there more than one person in the house seeing strange things?

5. Is more than one person hearing voices or strange sounds?

6. Are personal items being found in strange places?

7. Are personal items missing?

8. Do strange things happen during the day?

9. Do strange things happen at the same time every day or night?

10. Does everyone in the house as well as visitors to the home feel like they are not alone even if they are?

11. When you are taking pictures in the house, do strange anomalies show up in the pictures?

12. Do you have strange occurrences with electric orbattery operated items in your house?

13. Do your pets react to things you can't see or hear?

If you answered YES to eight or more of these questions, then I feel your house is really haunted. Now it is up to you to find out whom or what is causing the activity.

We will get to that later in the book.

WHY IS MY HOUSE HAUNTED?

This is a question many people asked themselves. There are a multitude of reasons. They range from the house itself. All the way, to the history of the area where it is built. In this chapter, I will try to help you uncover some of these mysteries.

You have now moved into an old house. You soon notice some pretty strange things happening. The first thing you need to realize is, there have been many people in this house over the years. Any one of those people's spirits could be haunting your home. It could be the people who built their dream house. It could be former owners or renters. It could even be a spirit of a person who visited the home and loved it. The next thing you need to do is find out why they are there. This is when you do a history on your old house. I will tell you how later.

Well, that's all fine and dandy for the people who live in old houses. What if you live in a brand new house that is haunted? How could this happen? Nobody has lived in it but you. It could be the land on which it was built. Don't worry! Your children aren't going to be sucked through the old color TV set after the national anthem plays at midnight!

You now need to find out what happened on that land years ago. Was there a former building there? It could be it was once home to Native Americans. There are hundreds of reasons properties can be haunted, this is when you need to find out about your lands past life. This will be something that will help you in the future. I will show you how to do this very soon.

There is one more peculiar reason I will touch on. Your house may be a passageway. Think of it like a lobby of a hotel. People come and go, but they don't stay long. Some spirits may be lost and wondering the earth. They come into your house then continue their journey. It could be that there was once a road or some kind of path that cut through where your house now stands. Those spirits may just be going about their day not even know your house is there. There are so many reasons this happens. If you think your house is a passageway for wandering spirits, it is up to you to find out why.

My old stone house is a passageway for many spirits. I capture numerous spirits on my camera that really don't have anything to do with my house or property's history. I know being a sensitive, I attract spirits. Plus, I live really close to a grave yard. This may also have something to do with the passageway ghosts in my house.

These are just some of the reasons why spirits come in to my house or yours.

These spirits come in, sit a spell, see what's going on, and then leave once again. I have never had a passageway ghost stick around for long, I'm not saying they can't come in and stay for periods of time. I just know they never have in my experiences with them. I really can't explain why this happens. I just know some people witness it and can't explain it.

The best way to expose some of these hauntings is to do a complete history of your house, your land, and the area in which your house stands. This is what I will illustrate in the chapter titled: Know Your History.

I know what you are thinking.....

Oh No! Research! Well, don't take on so. Relax! I will explain how to go about it in a simple manner.

It really is very easy, informative, and fun too!

INTELLIGENT HAUNTING OR RESIDUAL HAUNTING

Did you know there are different types of haunting? You may have an intelligent haunting. Or, your house may have a residual haunting taking place.

An intelligent haunting is where the ghosts can interact with the living. You may hear knocks or things turning on by themselves. You may feel a cold touch or hear them whisper your name in your ear. These types of haunting are usually caused by spirits of people who have not yet crossed over. Either by choice or because they think they have unfinished business in this world. An intelligent haunting can also be caused by spirits who just feel like they still own your home, which was once theirs. They were once very happy there and just don't want to leave. They could also believe this will always be their home and you are the trespassers.

Intelligent hauntings are sometimes stirred up by renovations or even small changes in the home, like moving furniture around or bringing in company. I know my ghosts don't like change at all. Big or small. One tilts my pictures on the wall to the right when she is upset. Another will steal our guest's keys. He will return them only when he is asked.

Some spirits may also get riled up if there is a lot of negativity or strife between family members. In my house everything I just stated, changes in weather, and other natural causes, make the activity much higher than normal.

These types of hauntings can sometimes be calmed by setting boundaries or rules the spirits must follow to be a cohabitant with you. If you really want them out, which is not an easy task to undertake, a house cleansing ceremony may help make your home calmer and feel lighter. Remember, It is not a guarantee that they will leave. Some spirits are very stubborn! Especially, if they were so in life. I will explain both of these techniques and how to perform them later in the book.

A residual haunting is something entirely different. It is like a movie or tape recorder being played on a loop over and over again. This type of haunting is usually caused by an incident that happened years ago. Either in the home or, on the land on which it was built. The energy of that event has imprinted into the space in which it happened and is locked there forever.

You will be able recognize this type of haunting by seeing or hearing the same things happening in the same places every time. For example, if you hear footsteps going down the hallway, then a door close every night at 10:00 pm. This is more than likely an energy imprint of this event. Sometime during your home's history, someone took this path every night to go to bed. Or, something tragic may have happened, and this was the last walk that person took before their death. The spirits and the events have imprinted their energy into the hallway and it just plays back over and over again. Like a looped recording.

Unfortunately, there is really nothing you can do about a residual haunting. You can try a house cleansing to see if you can clear any negative energies if there was a tragedy in your home. But, if it is just

"Old Mrs. Smith" going through her nightly routine and walking down the hall every night at ten. It is just something you will just have to get used to.

Objects in the home may hold residual energy too. If you bring a new item into your home and paranormal activity stirs up, that item may be to blame. Be sure to cleanse any antique or personal item such as jewelry, mirrors, etc. You can leave them in the sun all day or smudge them with sage smoke. If salt won't ruin the item, soak it in sea salt water. You can also bury it in dry sea salt and leave it in the sun for a few hours. These are the best ways I know of to cleanse personal items that may hold energy. I'm not saying you should take everything out of your house and let it bake in the sun. Just keep an eye out for strange activity if a new item is brought into your home.

Also, if you already own an antique or another used item and you notice it may be the cause of your haunting. Remove it from your house and cleanse it well. If the activity continues when the item is returned, I would suggest getting rid of it all together, but only if the activity is so strong you can't handle it. If you decide to sell it or give it to someone else, please disclose your strange experiences you had with the item while you owned it.

It not a law you have to do so, but it is the right thing to do!

ENVIRONMENTAL FACTORS THAT MAY AMPLIFY ACTIVITY

When I was researching the history of my property, I ran into some very interesting information I had never realized before. The reason my house is so active is due to some of the environmental factors on the surrounding the property.

First of all, I live on a mountain in a stone house. I found out that certain types of rocks like limestone, shale, quarts, and granite, can absorb and hold residual energies in them. The energy from past events that may have occurred on your property imprints into the rocks and is held there forever. My house sits right on top of an ancient mountain that is full of deposits of these very stones. My home also has stone siding.

I also came across information about water. Running water can stir up paranormal activity. I have a creek and underground springs on my property. Running water can carry energy. This also may be the cause for some of my "pathway ghosts." Their energy follows the running water that passes under and around my home. Fast moving bodies of water can also produce enough energy that spirits can tap into to help them manifest. If you live along the coast, ocean tides can do the same.

Wind is also a factor. There is a breeze blowing constantly up here. High winds can stir up activity just like water can, by producing energy for the spirits to draw on. You may notice a change in the energy level within your home when the wind is higher than normal.

Moon cycles can also cause the paranormal activity to ramp up. Full moons and new moons carry a lot of energy. They cause higher tides, and more animal movement in forests. It is also the time when more criminal acts happen in this world, and on a lighter note, when more babies are born in the hospitals. If moon cycles can cause all of this to happen. Isn't it highly possible for them to cause your house to go crazy with activity too?

Thunderstorms are a huge factor in the paranormal world. They don't only set a spooky atmosphere within your haunted house; they also hold a lot of power. The storm itself is charged with energy. When the lightning strikes it actually ionizes the air. This is the perfect environment for ghosts to draw energy. I have captured some of my best paranormal evidence over the years during thunderstorms.

I have only touched on a few of the environmental factors that may be causing the paranormal events to amplify in your home. Next time you feel like your house is going nuts, write down the factors that may be causing the unnatural events. Is there a full moon? Or is there a bad storm brewing in the distance.

Once you start to understand some of the underlying factors that may be causing the spirits to act up more than they normally do, you can ease your mind a little bit. Knowing wholeheartedly the temporary flare-up of otherworldly events won't last forever.

WHAT YOU MAY BE WITNESSING

Spirits have many ways of showing themselves to you. It could be anything from a tiny flash of light to a full blown apparition. They will also let you know through knocks, bumps, whistles, singing and other unexplained noises. I will try to explain what you may be witnessing in your house. I have come across many of these manifestations in my own home. For me, and my family, seeing and hearing strange things have become part of our everyday lives.

Visuals

Orbs: Orbs are the most controversial phenomena in the paranormal world. Most people think they are just dust particles, bugs, or water vapors that are floating in the air and the only time you can see them is if light strikes them the right way. Others believe they are actual spirit energies that form in the shape of spheres. Some people also believe, orbs occur right before a spirit tries to manifest. It is the way it draws energy from the surrounding atmosphere to gain strength. Orbs can be seen in many different colors. I have seen orbs with my naked eye, and I know for a fact they were not caused by a bug or dust! Most of the time, this type of spirit energies will go unnoticed.

Spirit / Ghost Lights: Spirit or Ghost Lights can be seen in many different forms and colors. They may show as solid orbs, flashing strobe lights, or you just may catch a flash of light out of the corner of your eye. You might see these lights in the form of tiny sparks, flitting around the room. These are sometimes called Sprites All of these forms of spirit or ghost lights are the energy of a ghost trying to gain enough strength to manifest. Usually they can only muster up enough energy to cause a quick flash of light.

Mists: Mists can form when a spirit is trying to appear. This again is an energy mass that has been gathered by an entity. They can show in all colors. Dark or black mists usually mean a darker energy is present. If you see mists in your home try to debunk it before chalking it up to paranormal activity. It could be condensation within the house that has formed around drafty areas on a cold day or from an air conditioning unit that has just been turned on.

Rods: Rods are straight beams of light. They may be seen as a single light or in a formation. These are also spirits trying to gain enough energy to show themselves. These rods may be seen coming from the walls, ceiling, or may floating in mid air. Rods may be seen in an array of different colors.

Shadows: Shadows are full body apparitions. They are solid and very dark. They can be seen in the shape of a mass or as a human like figure. Shadows usually indicate a darker entity is in your presence, but this is not always the case. This could be a human spirit that cannot draw enough strength to manifest into a full blown apparition that may show color and recognizable features.

Partial Apparitions: Partial Apparitions are seen in many forms. You may only see a part of the body such as arms, legs, the head, or just half of the body. Usually these form as white or in gray tones. Very rarely do you see an apparition of this sort in a solid form. Most of the sightings seem wispy, misty, or smoky. This is caused when the spirit has gained enough strength to truly show themselves as a human figure with features you can recognize.

Full Body Apparitions: Some paranormal investigators call this the "holy grail of ghost sightings" Very rarely does anyone see a full body apparition. This is when the ghost has gained enough power to actually show itself in full human form. You will see the distinguishing features of a person, like the hair and eyes. You also may be able to make out the clothing or even the jewelry the ghost is wearing. They may show themselves in a misty gray or white formation. Or, if you are one of the truly lucky ones you will see it in full blown color! It may be transparent or it may be solid. Either way, if you do witness a full body apparition consider yourself privileged.

Audio

Knocks and Bangs: Knocks and bangs could be caused by environmental factors within or outside of your house. The foundation may be settling or the wood flooring may be expanding or contracting due to the weather conditions outside. Heating and cooling of the air inside the home may also cause this phenomenon. Spirits can cause knocking and banging sounds too. This is an easy way they can show their presence. If you hear these knocks and bangs at the same time every day, it could be from a residual haunting. If you hear knocking and you knock or bang back, and get a repetitive response, you are probably dealing with an intelligent spirit. Before you decide it is definite paranormal activity, be sure to debunk any other thing that may be causing the noise.

Disembodied Voices: These are also rare occurrences. Especially, if you hear them with your own ears. Most of the time they will show up on special paranormal devices called ghost boxes or on digital recordings. You may hear these as a faint whisper, a normal speaking voice, or as a scream. In our home we have heard singing, grumbles, and our names being called from a distance.

Disembodied voices can be from an intelligent spirit in your house or from an imprinted event from log ago.

Footsteps: This is pretty self explanatory. Footsteps can be heard from intelligent spirits within your home or from a residual haunting.

Other Experiences You May Have

Cold/ Hot Spots: These pockets of hot or cold air can be caused by entities trying to show themselves. It is thought they pull the energies from the atmosphere around the spot to give them more power to manifest. This can also be caused by natural factors. Please check for drafts and heating or cooling sources in the area of the anomaly.

Goose bumps: Goose bumps are a natural reaction of the hair follicles when the body comes in contact with a cooler environment. In the paranormal world it is thought to be caused by coming in contact with a spirit. You could also feel the hairs on your body stand up. This is due to an electric charge or static in the air around your body. Ghosts are known to produce this type of energy.

Touches: Sometimes intelligent spirits feel the need to reach out and touch you. This up close and personal experience is another uncommon occurrence. I have only been touch twice in my life time. It is a very unnerving and I don't like it at all!

If this does happen to you, tell the entity in a very stern voice, that it is not acceptable to touch you or others in your house at anytime. This will usually take care of the problem.

Darker Occurrences

If you are hearing growls, hisses, or heavy scratching sounds within your home, you are probably dealing with a dark entity. These negative energies have also been known to deeply scratch, burn, and hit people. They have been reported to throw or break objects. These are very violent beings! If this is sounds even remotely familiar to you, please reach out to someone who can come in and remove this dark energy or being from your home as soon as possible! It is not something you want in your home, and it is definitely not anything to play around with! Try to ignore and avoid contact of any kind with dark beings.

These are just a few of the spectral occurrences you may witness. Please be sure to try to find worldly causes for these anomalies before you chalk it up to paranormal activity! Scratching in the walls may be a rodent or bats in your attic. Disembodied voices could be a neighbor's voice carried on the wind. Go over every possible explanation. If you still can't find a good source for the noise, voice, light, etc., then it could be a spirit!

Paranormal Activity is an unknown and unpredictable world of its own. If your home anything like mine, you are always going to be wondering what kind of freaky event is going to happen next! Don't worry, there are techniques to clam the spirits and gain control of your home once again. We will get to that very soon!

WHY ARE YOU SENSINGSTRANGE THINGS WHEN OTHERS AROUND YOU AREN'T?

I'm sure you have asked yourself this question many times. I know I did for many years. Until, I finally discovered that I am a sensitive. Otherwise known as, a medium. This is a person, who is more in tune with their surroundings, and are able to pick up on certain things others may not. Such as, paranormal activity.

I am able to see, hear, and feel spirits. I have always had this ability. My daughter is an empath. She can feel energies around her and pick up on other's pain. Especially, the pain in animals. She can also hear sprits. My son has all of my abilities. He is still young he has not fully developed his gifts but, he knows he has these abilities and accepts them. I have always been open with my children about the paranormal and their gifts ever since they were very young. I am truly thankful that now you can say things like "I see ghosts" or

"I live in a haunted house", and people accept it more openly!

Now, are you a sensitive?

Here is a check list to find out.

1. Have you ever heard a voice when nobody was there?

2. Have you ever seen something you couldn't explain?

3. Are you able to feel other's pain or emotions?

4. Do you ever have dajavu?

5. Do you ever have vivid dreams that come true?

6. Do you ever feel like someone is watching you when nobody is there?

7. Do you ever feel like something is going to happen in the near future and it does?

8. Do you have a very keen intuition?

9. Are you a "night owl"?

10. Are you a very creative person?

If you answered YES to seven or more of these questions you are probably a sensitive!

It is thought that these gifts are passed down from the mother's side of the family. If your mom or grandmother had these abilities, then you probably will too. It is nothing to be ashamed about. It is just something you need to do some research on and learn to use them to the best of your ability.

Through my own research I have noticed that people who suffer from debilitating migraine headaches may be gifted. I suffer from debilitating migraine headaches and have since I was about fifteen years old. My children also suffer from this evil, mind bending, pain. When I say debilitating, I mean you can do nothing but lie still in a dark room with no noise what so ever. Even a kitten purring at the bottom of the bed will sound like a freight train in the room. Thankfully, my son recovers quickly. It is a whole other story for me and my daughter. We may fight the pain for days on end. I am not going to claim this as true science. But, I have talked to many other people who are gifted through the years, and they also have said they suffer with migraines. So, there just may be something to this crazy theory. There are ways to take control of your gifts. It takes time to learn these techniques. But, in the long run it is something you really need to do.

The first thing is to empower yourself. Try to control your fear.

Some spirits thrive on your fear. If you feel like you are getting overwhelmed by energies. Tell them to back off and leave you alone. Always use a stern voice and truly mean what you say!

You also need to protect yourself. This is how I do it. Visualize a bright light surrounding you from your toes to the top of your head. Incase yourself in this light and declare out loud that you are protected. I call it my personal space bubble. I use it with living people as well as with spirits. Let the spirits know wholeheartedly that they are never allowed in your bubble! I do this whenever I feel spirits around me and I do not wish to be bothered at that time.

Next, try to keep yourself in a calm environment. I know when I get over stimulated I get very annoyed. My house stays very quiet. I get overwhelmed with loud noises. Such as, loud music, non stop talking, and just general chaos. If you find yourself feeling this way, remove yourself from the noise and take some slow deep breaths. Then, if you have to return to the loud space, do it only when you feel calm and collected. Let others around you know that it is not the company it is just you, and you, needed to get some air. I know this sounds really selfish, but we ARE different than most people. To stay mentally stable we really need to take care of ourselves and not worry about what other people think. If you want to explain the reason you walked away in further detail you can. But, I will leave that up to you.

The last thing I would suggest is to find other people who have these gifts and talk to them. I have found a lot of people online that are true mediums. You can talk with them and see what they are going through and learn from them. This is how I got to know that I was a true sensitive years ago.

I liked the online approach. I could talk to other people who had gifts without someone looking directly at me. I never felt judged. If there are people are judging you, then you are talking to the wrong people. Again, do your own research. Look for books on the subject or find reliable web sites. You just might be amazed what you find out about yourself and your wonderful gifts!

E.M.F. SENSITIVITY

E.M.F stands for Electro Magnetic Fields. They can come from natural sources and manmade devices. Some people are highly sensitive to these fields. It is also believed in the paranormal world, that spirits emit these energies when they are trying to communicate or manifest.

There are many natural sources of E.M.F. Certain rocks and minerals can give of E.M.F. Such as, limestone, quartz, granite, and slate. Water is another source. Fast moving water has been shown to produce these fields. Ground water is highly charged with E.M.F. This is how "water witches" or dowers find water in the ground for wells. They use dowsing sticks or rods that will cross when they detect the E.M.F. the water is producing deep within the earth. Another natural origin of E.M.F is caused by vortexes in the earth. Arizona has many of these natural vortexes. Many people go there for healing and cleansing from this powerful earth energy. It has also been shown that trees that have been struck by lightning will a give off high E.M.F. readings.

Man made E.M.F is around us all the time. It is produced by our computers, fuse boxes, heating/cooling units, breaker boxes, coffee machines, television sets, and the list goes on and on.

Basically, anything that is electrical in our homes has an electromagnetic field around it. The bigger the device or appliance, the higher the E.M.F. reading will be. Even the wiring in our homes produces an electromagnetic field. If any of the wiring is faulty, it could produce even more of these invisible waves of electricity.

There are many people who are highly sensitive to these fields. The very young and the very old show a heightened sensitivity in lab tests. Some people who suffer from migraine headaches and other medical conditions that deal with the brain may be even more susceptible. These symptoms may include dizziness, headaches, nausea, and paranoia.

Sometimes in extreme cases, electromagnetic fields can cause people to hallucinate. If you are having any of these symptoms in your home, don't worry. There are things that can be done to combat high E.M.F.

The first thing to try is to have an electrician come into your home and check for any high readings that may be causing your symptoms. They have special devices that can detect where the problem may be radiating from. If there is nothing detected by these readings, you can try unplugging some of the appliances and devices you don't use very often. This will cut down on the discharge of E.M.F. into your living space. You should start feeling better soon after you do this. Another way to cut down on these toxic waves is to have potted plants in your home. They help absorb and cleanse the atmosphere of the electrical pollution. Placing them in areas that contain a lot of electrical gear will help with this vexing issue

TALKING TO YOUR CHILDREN

When it comes to talking to your children about the paranormal, it all comes down to you. I don't know your kids. I can't give you exact instructions on how to do this, or even how to approach the subject. The only thing I can do is tell you how I talked to mine. You can use it as a guide. You know your kids better than anyone. How they react in situations, their feelings, and how much of an imagination they might have. I will tell you the secret though. The golden key to unlock all of this is....

Honesty Is The Best Policy!

Kids these days are a lot smarter then we give them credit for. With paranormal shows on just about every cable channel, and easy internet access everywhere, kids know a lot. They see and hear things we thought were unimaginable when we were young. Don't lie to them, they will catch you and bust you on the spot! Then you will lose their trust. I know it sounds daunting, but it's a lot easier then explaining the birds and the bees!

I have always been sensitive to the paranormal world. When I was growing up, talk of such things was a huge taboo. You were either considered an odd child, or people just thought you had lost your mind completely. So, I kept all of my experiences and gifts to myself.

I decided a long time ago, that if or when I had children of my own, this would be an open topic in my family. No secrets, no lies, or whatevers. If my children were gifted like I am, they would understand everything they needed to know. I promised myself they would never be scared and afraid to talk about what they experience like I was. I never dreamed I would have two with gifts almost as strong as mine!

When my children started coming to me with questions about some of the "scary" things they saw at night I really wasn't surprised. The first thing

I did was calm them down. It is a lot easier talk to someone who is calm and not out of their head crazy with fear. I would ask them what they saw, what happened when they saw it, and what their reaction was to the experience. Then we would talk about what may have caused it. Could it have been a shadow from a tree outside? Could it have been headlights from a passing car? If the answer was no, then we would try to figure out what it actually was.

I would have them describe exactly what they saw in detail. In my house since we did our history, we sort of know "who" it is. Then we talk about why the spirit may have done what they experienced. We would talk about it openly and try to figure out what to do next. Most of the time just letting them "talk it out" comforted them enough that they went back to what they were doing before that had their encounter.

The last thing you want to do is ignore what your child encountered. You may think it is just their imagination, but to them it could be very real! They rely on you to be the ones they can go to with their problems, fears, and questions. If you don't know what is going on in your house, do some research. This is where doing a history comes in really handy. Let your kids help you with the research. It may help them answer some of their own questions.

Especially, if they are hesitant to talk to anyone about the paranormal activity they have been witnessing.

If you think it really is just an excuse not to go to bed, or an attention getting ploy, I have a wonderful answer for that situation. Purchase a can of "Ghost Spray"! What? It is a simple can of air freshener! This works really well with young children (2 -5). Explain to the child that ghosts don't like smell good spray. They will run away if they smell it because they think it stinks! Before bed, walk around the room with the child and spray the corners, under the bed, and please never forget the spooky closet!

You can make up a rhyme like:

Ghostly spirits in this room,

Disappear in this stinky plume!

Recite it over and over with the child
as you spray the room.

I know, this is a BIG FAT LIE, and I
said to always tell children the truth
about paranormal activity. This is
something you can try **ONLY** if you
know there is absolutely no
paranormal activity in your house. If
you do experiment with the "ghost
spray" and your child is still having
scary encounters, then you really need
to have a long and honest talk about
what is really going on in your home.

Remember, always be truthful with your child and never doubt what they have experienced. Just because YOU haven't seen or heard anything in your home, doesn't mean that the ghosts aren't really there! Do your research and the most important thing is...Always Be a Good Listener!

TALKING WITH OTHERS

Most of the time, people don't like to talk about their encounters. They feel like people will judge them or think they are crazy. As I have stated many times before, when I was a child I didn't talk about the things I experienced at all. If I did it was only with my brother or very close friends I could trust.

Now days, it's a normal conversation people may have over coffee. The paranormal world has opened up so much over the past few years that it is not a forbidden subject anymore. I will give you an example:

My husband was at the doctor's office, and ran into the man who used to live in our house as a child. The man asked him if the house was still haunted. My husband told him it was, and struck up a conversation about some of the things we've seen and heard. He also told him that so many things had happened that I was in the middle of writing a book about them.

A little old lady was also sitting in the waiting room. She overheard their conversation, and started telling my husband about her paranormal experiences. My husband said she didn't look like somebody who would even believe in ghosts; much less tell her story to a complete stranger.

This is what I am talking about. If someone hears your story, they may feel comfortable enough to open up and tell you theirs, or, visa versa. The timing is the thing you need to remember. Don't blurt out in church or in line at the grocery store that you see ghosts. This probably won't go over too well. Instead, look for an opportunity to open up so you can discuss your experiences. You may over hear a conversation, like the little lady did. Or, you may be at a bookstore and see someone looking in the paranormal section. These are perfect occasions to strike up a conversation about spirits.

If you still aren't comfortable talking to others face to face, there are plenty of places online. Look for web sites that have discussion boards or chats. You can also find pages you can post your ghost pictures or stories on and tag them. I have talked to a lot of people just by doing this very thing.

Just remember, today the world is more open to bizarre things then it used to be. Ease into the subject. Then when you feel comfortable go for it! You will be surprised how many people have a story just like you do, and were afraid to tell anyone until you came along!

KNOW YOUR HISTORY

The best way to know who or what is sharing your home with you is to do a complete history of your house. I know this sounds like a huge undertaking, but it is something you can include the whole family in. Yes, it does take a lot of time and sometimes you will run into dead ends (excuse the pun!). But, this will be very helpful with other things I will discuss in the book. Trust me. It is worth the effort.

You can start, like I did, by contacting former owners or renters. Ask if they know anything historical pertaining to your home. Be sure to ask about the possibility of old out buildings that are no longer standing. Old wells and anything else they may know about that involves your home or property. If you feel like they are opened minded, ask if they ever had anything strange happen in the house while they lived there. You may be surprised when they volunteer information about their paranormal experiences before you even bring it up. Find out all the details you can of deaths in the house or on the land. Families, which may have formally lived in the home, and any tragedies that may have happened in the home or on the property. Pay attention to every little detail. Sometimes they are your best clues. If you can't find anyone willing to give out information, which is a good possibility, you can look for resources at your local historical society, library, and courthouse. Deeds, marriage certificates, death certificates, and burial records are all public record. This information could lead you to web sites containing even more answers. I know this sounds like a lot to do, but you will find out in the end, it is worth every minute. Don't ever give up. Take your time and enjoy your journey through the years.

After you complete all of your research, you might find out why your house is haunted and who is sharing it with you. Just think! With all of your new found knowledge, the experiences you are having may start making more since. I have found that you will also start to become more in tune with your surroundings. The most amazing thing is, you could find out the spirits have a really good reason to be there, and it's not so creepy and scary after all!

NOW WHAT DO I DO?

Ok, you have done your research. You have now determined that you really are living in a haunted house. You and others in the home are seeing, hearing, and feeling things you just can't explain. What do you do now?

After moving to The Old Stone House in Tennessee fourteen years ago, I decided to start taking down notes. I grabbed an old notebook that was left over from the former school year. Every time something strange happened in the house I would jot down a detailed description of the event. The following is one of my actual notes.

6/1/11 8:00 pm I heard the front storm door bang like my husband was home and hitting it to come in. The dog and cat also heard it and reacted to the sudden bang. I went to open it thinking my husband would be on the other side ... and nothing was there. The house was very hot and beside the door it was cool like air conditioning was blowing. About 2 minutes later I saw a white flash of lines go from the edge of the sofa arm past the door. This happened again two nights later.

It sounds like a lot of work for nothing. But, it really helped us in the long run.

We used all the gathered information to find out what was really going on in our home. We also used it to put two and two together and figured out who was haunting it.

This is my method for great note taking. Think of yourself as a roving reporter and start with the basics.

The five "W's".

WHO did it happen to?

WHAT actually happened?

WHEN did it happen?

WHERE did it happen?

WHY did it happen?

The last one is always the hardest one to answer. Always try to debunk the event before you chalk it up to paranormal activity. For example, if you feel a cold breeze looks for a source that may have caused it. An open window, a crack under the door, etc. If you can't find a really good explanation then it could be paranormal. If you do debunk the event, write that down too. That way if it happens again you will know it's not a ghost in your midst.

If you decide to start taking notes like I did, you must do it every time you have a strange occurrence. Even if it is a tiny knock that happens every three days. It is a important piece of evidence. This type of documentation can be very valuable for future use.

What if you have had experiences in the past, but never thought to write them down? Don't worry about it! You can still record them. Try to remember them as clearly as you can. If some memories are faded, jot down what you do recall. Then walk away from it. You may recollect a few more items to add later. Remember, a partial note is better than no notes at all!

So..... What are you waiting for? Go grab that old notebook and get started!!!

TAKING CONTROL OF YOUR HOME

Why do I feel like I have lost control of my house to these spirits? I know you may have asked this question at one point in a moment of fear. You moved into a beautiful house and now you feel like you are not the owner anymore! This is how you can change that feeling once and for all.

If you feel comfortable, gather your family into the center room of the house. Light a *white candle* and place it in the room somewhere it can stay lit all night. Be sure it is out of the reach of children and pets and in a fireproof container. Say a prayer of your choice and ask for protection for everyone who is present. Have the strongest person in the home state out loud in a very stern voice:

"This is our house now! We all know you were here first. But, it is our family's home now! You can stay if you want or you may choose to leave with this white light.

If you do decide to stay, you must not show yourself in any way to anyone that lives here or comes into this house! You may not interact with the children or animals! You may not make noises, lights, or any other signs of your presence!

If any of these rules are broken, you will be forced out!"

Leave the white candle burning until it burns out on its own. This may take a few hours. Again, be sure it is in * a fire proof container* and on a fire proof surface. Also be sure that it is out of the reach of children and pets.

After the flame burns out, bury the wax stump somewhere off of your property. You may also throw it into a creek, river, ocean, or lake. By doing this, if the spirit decided to leave your home with the white light, it can now be released.

If you do not feel comfortable involving the whole family you may do the same procedure on your own.

The key to this is to say it with feeling and mean what you say!

Now, what if the same thing keeps happening? Just remember most spirits you encounter were once human. Some people need to be reminded over and over again. If they start acting up again, just strictly remind them of the rules. Be patient! Things should start calming down soon after you state the rules of your home. If your house is still of the charts with activity, don't worry! We will cover that in the next chapter!

I always use a white votive candle that will fit in a small Mason jar. I dispose of the jar and spent wax in the creek beside my house.

Cleansing Your Home

Does your house ever feel sad? Does the home seem dark and the air thick and heavy? Is your spirit activity overwhelming your home and family? Then it is time to do a house cleansing. I try to do this at least every six months. I will also do it if there is a lot of tension between family members and when the activity seems to be heightening in my home.

This is a very easy, but serious way to cleanse your house of negative energies. It only takes a short amount of time to do and it will make your home feel lighter and brighter soon after you complete the process. First you need to gather your supplies.

You will need:

Sea Salt

1 Sage Smug Stick

1 White Candle with a Fireproof Holder

Lavender Water in a spray bottle

An empty jar to extinguish the smudge stick

If you do not feel you can find all of the supplies needed for the cleansing in your shopping area.

Or, you are reluctant to go shop for the supplies. I do have a house cleansing kits available. You may order one directly from me by contacting my web address. This is located in: A Message to my Readers section, at the end of the book.

Each kit has full written instructions. It has been purified and charged during the full moon and the following day in full sun to achieve full effectiveness. All of the kits are beautifully packaged and have been created, charged, and hand packed personally. The candle and smudge stick are both handcrafted. The beautiful candle in my kit contains special essential oils and herbs to help support the process.

No outside hands will touch the contents until you have opened it to cleanse your home. Each House Cleansing Kit is $ 45.00 US.(This price includes all shipping charges and tax.)

Let's get started:

Please read through this carefully before you start. You must follow the directions as they are written.

DO NOT SKIP ANYTHING!

This is a very serious undertaking and must be done by the letter to attain the desired outcome.

Do Not try to perform this cleansing by yourself! Have someone with you at all times. Remember, there is power in numbers!

IF AT ANYTIME YOU FEEL UNCOMFORTABLE, STOP

AND GET OUT OF THE HOUSE!

This situation may be too much for you to handle on your own. Please seek outside help if this happens!

DO NOT SKIP ANYTHING!

THE CLENSING

1. Remove ALL the pets and young children from the home.

2. Open ALL the windows and doors.

This includes: cabinets, closets, crawl spaces, etc.

3. Place a jar of water on your front porch or steps.

4. Say a prayer of protection of your choice.

5. Take a fire proof container and set it in the center of the home, on a heat proof surface, safe from pets and children. Pour a small amount of salt (about 1/4 inch) into the bottom of the container. Place the white candle in the center of the salt. Light the candle and say in a **commanding tone:**

*** "I fill this house with light and love!

All negative energies must leave now!

You are not welcome in my home!"

6. Light the end of the sage wand. Blow on it gently until it is smoking continuously.

*** Again state the above in a commanding voice!

7. Go room to room with the smoking sage.

Being very sure the smoke gets into Every nook and cranny.

*** Repeating, out loud, over and over, the above statement!

8. Go outside and let the smoke clear from the house.

Slowly sweep the sage stick from the tip of your toes to the top of your head, allowing the smoke to fully surround your body. Be sure to let your partner do the same. You may also wave it over each other in turn.

Place the smudge stick in the jar of water you set outside your home. Leave this jar on your porch.

Take deep breaths of fresh air to clear your body. Think positive thoughts to clear your mind.

Say a prayer of thanks of your choice.

9. Return to the house. *Do Not Shut The Doors or Windows!* Go around the

home tossing a pinch of sea salt into the open closets and other spaces,

State: "This space is now purified!"

Shutting the doors, when the salt has been dispersed.

10. Again, Take the sea salt and sprinkle a pinch on each window sill and close the window stating:

"This window is now sealed from negative energies crossing into my home!"

Repeat until every window is closed in the house.

11. Go to the outside doors. Sprinkle a line of salt across the threshold,

Stating: "This doorway is now sealed from any Negative Energies crossing into my home!"

Firmly shut the door.

12. Let the white candle burn out on its own. This may take a few hours. When the flame goes out, Take the spent wax and the remaining salt outside to the jar with the smudge stick in it. Place the spent wax and salt into the jar of water. Take the jar of "unclean" supplies off your property and bury it, or throw it into a body of water.

This is the final step. Your house should feel much lighter and brighter.

Refresh and Revitalize

Take the lavender water and spray it into each room. This will refresh and revive your home you have just reclaimed!

There are no guarantees that this will remove the negative energies from your home!

It is something you can try to see if it works for you. If you think it has been effective, then this process should be repeated every six months or when you feel it is needed.

If you still feel a negative presence in your home and you have tried this cleansing several times. Please seek some reputable outside help from your religious leader, congregation, or other source. This being may need more then sage and salt to drive it out!

NEGATIVE ENERGIES AND DARK SPIRITS

I have cleansed my house and set down the rules, but nothing has changed. What do I do now? If the cleansing ceremony hasn't worked you may be dealing with very strong dark or negative energies. These beings can show themselves as shadows, dark mists, or by causing problems with one or more person in the home. You may see personality changes or there could be a lot of fighting over little things. This is the type of energy these dark spirits feed on. This is something I have never come across. I would suggest that you should get some outside help.

You can turn to your church or other religious groups that perform house blessings. This is done by using religious prayers and rites. You have to be very open and honest with them about what is going on. Don't be scared that they will think you are crazy. Most of these people have heard it all. They shouldn't judge you if you are seeking their help. If they are judgmental, then walk away. You don't need any more stress. If they are going to help you, they have to know everything! This is where your history comes in handy. Let them take a look at it and see if they can figure what may be causing the negative energies you have reported.

If you think it is a demonic entity in your home, you must contact someone who is very educated in this field. Do not try to interact with this evil being. The demon may present itself as a kind ghost, just to turn on you later. You may find scratches on your body. Usually they look like three cat scratches or bad sunburn. Another thing that may show a demon is afoot is, you may just feel depressed for no good reason.

This is very important! Please don't fall for someone out of the blue, who is going to charge you huge amounts of money, or even do it for free to come in and perform an exorcism. It won't work! Only a Catholic Priest can perform a TRUE exorcism. It can only be done if ordered by the Catholic Church itself. This can take a very long time to be approved if it is at all. Do some research and see if this is what is happening in your home. Contact a Priest. He will know how to get the Catholic Church involved if needed. Remember, you have to be honest and open about what is happening in your home.

Now, just because you have a negative spirit in your house it doesn't mean it is evil or a demon. It just might be a spirit who had a very hard life while that person was alive. Everyone knows someone who is negative all the time, or a grumpy old man that lives in the neighborhood.

The irate spirit in your house may just be one of those people. A lot of these spirits are very stubborn and hard to clear from the living environment. Especially, if they were stubborn in life. You may want to call in a local paranormal investigation team to see if they can identify this spirit. I will tell you how to go about this in the next chapter.

Try the house cleansing again. This time address the negative spirit very strongly. If you know his or her identity, use it. Let it know you are not going to put up with their negativity in your home and that they must leave now! Scream it if you have to. Let this spirit know, without out a doubt, this is your home now and they are not welcome under any circumstance. If this still doesn't take care of your problem please contact someone who truly understands the situation and let them aid in removing this spirit.

Please don't ever become discouraged. Just because you need to ask for assistance doesn't mean you're weak or doing something wrong. You can't always handle everything on your own, and that is perfectly ok! Don't suffer with a negative or dark spirit in your home. Seek out reputable help if you need it!

PARANORMAL
INVESTIGATIONS

If you are really concerned, scared, or feel your haunting could cause you harm, look into contacting a reputable paranormal investigative team. Ladies, please don't be surprised, if three very hot guys don't appear at your beautiful home to investigate. This is not television! Most of the time, the people that show up at your door are just regular, open minded, people from your community or a surrounding area.

You can find a local group in your area on the internet, and believe it or not, in the phonebook! Look over their web site then e-mail your concerns or call them on the phone and tell them about your situation. They will contact you soon after.

Ask a lot of questions during the phone interview and be honest. Remember, this is what these groups deal with all the time. If you feel like the team is qualified to handle your case, schedule a public, face to face meeting. Once you talk to them you will know if you will continue with them or not. Be sure to ask how many investigations they have done. Ask to see results from a previous case if possible, and ask about the kind of equipment they use to do their research.

After you decide the team is compatible with you and you're haunting. Hand over all of the notes you have taken and the complete history of your house and property. (See, I told you this would be handy for future use!) This will give your investigators all the information they will need to possibly unlock the mysteries of your haunting. Most local paranormal investigators go into the situation blindly. Your compiled information will help them immensely and they will probably be shocked that you are so prepared.

Each team has a certain way of doing things. Some like you to leave your home while they are there. While others like for you to participate. You will have to decide which method is right for you when you are choosing a team. Be sure to ask which method they use before allowing them to come into your home.

When the investigators arrive, they will tell you what you need to do, and set up their equipment all over your house. They will probably ask you where the highest level of activity happens in your home. This is so they can cover that area with more equipment and use their limited time more wisely.

After they finish up, you will probably have to wait a few weeks to receive your answers. This gives them time to review the evidence they may have captured and go over it slowly and thoroughly. Be prepared for the answers you might receive. They may find things you really don't want to know, or they may have not caught anything at all! It's not that they didn't try. It is because your ghosts decided not to respond. Don't get discouraged; you can always have another one done in the future with the same group or with a new one.

If you are having difficulty finding a team, as I did. Don't give up! Somewhere out there is a very special group of investigators who will be overjoyed to take on your case. Don't think there is something wrong with you or your home; it's just not the right time to have an investigation done. When the time is right the appropriate team will be there with bells on!

Having a paranormal investigation done in your home is a huge decision and should not be done hastily. Please know that it will stir up your activity a few days before it is scheduled to take place, and after the fact. Be prepared for this to happen. Don't settle on the first team who comes along. Do your research and choose sensibly. Hopefully, with the help from a qualified group of ghost hunters you will get the much needed answers you are looking for!

BEWARE!!!

"I don't need an investigation. I can find out what is happing myself!" I know it is very tempting to use any means you can find to discover who is haunting your house. I assure you, this can cause even more problems if you do not know what you are dabbling with. Case in point: Ouija Boards and séances.

They are known as Ouija boards, Spirit boards, or Witch boards. These divining boards originated in Europe and became very popular in the mid 1800's when the spiritualist movement took hold in America. They would use these boards and séances to contact the dead. Real or fake, these mediums of that time made a lot of money! It is a well known fact that Mary Todd Lincoln went to these mediums to make contact her deceased children. Her husband President Lincoln was not impressed. He thought that is was a farce and they were taking advantage of his wife in her time of grief.

Ouija boards are made of wood or cardboard. They have the alphabet and the numbers 0-9 painted or printed on them. They also have a hello and a good bye point on them. There is also a separate piece called the planchete or pointer. This is what the person or people place the tips of their fingers on so that the spirits can use their energy to move it around the board. The planchete will move and point to different letters or numbers spelling out the answer to the questions asked. Thus, making contact with the spirit world whether it is with the good or the evil. The participants never know until it is too late!

I can hear you asking now, so, what's the big deal? Those boards are sold in toys stores in the game section. How can that be dangerous? Believe me, these spirit boards are not toys! They are portals to the other side. Sometimes when you open it you may invite unwelcome beings into your house. These unwelcome spirits may be more difficult to get rid of then you think. You may think you closed out the board and everything is fine, but sometimes the board doesn't close. This leaves the door wide open for spirits to cross over into your house at anytime!

Think of it as a door to a huge room. There are people in it that you know and trust and many you don't. You stand at the door and invite some people to come with you. Then before you know it, a couple of bad seeds stick their foot in the door preventing it from closing. They fall in, unnoticed; with the people you invited, and tag along before you realize you didn't shut the door all the way. It's not what you asked for, but it's what you got. This is exactly what can happen if you play with a spirit board. You can open a door you can't shut!

My advice is, Don't Ever Be Tempted to Use an Ouija Board. It is not worth it! They are not something you can control in any way. You may think you are speaking with a kind spirit and before you recognize your mistake; your house is out of control with very freaky paranormal activity. All because an unwelcome spirit came in while you were using the board! Besides, does it sound like a lot of fun having a spirit use your energy to move something? I would never ever allow that to happen and I hope you wouldn't either!

Séances are another activity I would advise you to avoid participating in. They can also bring very negative beings into your presences. How can this be so bad? It's just lighting a bunch of candles and joining hands around a table. Right? Wrong! It is a powerful ceremony that uses combined energy from the living to conjure ghosts to communicate and appear.

Back in the early days of séances, people flocked to mediums to have a chance to speak with their loved ones who crossed over. Most of the time it was all a trick by con artists to get rich. They would join hands while sitting in a pitch black room. Off to the side, there would be someone with a device to make the unknowing people think spirit voices were being heard. The table would shake, the clients were satisfied they made a connection, and the mediums would collect their money. I'm not saying that all mediums were fake. I'm sure some did have a true connection to the beyond. There were so many people claiming to be mediums at that time in history I'm pretty sure, the genuine ones were few and far between.

Séances are nothing to play around with either. They are very potent and can stir up paranormal activity to a level that can become out of control. Just because you finish the event doesn't mean everyone went home! You called on them purposely.

What happens if they thought it was an invitation to stay? Then you have more than just the spirit in your house you wanted to talk to. You have a big problem. Spirits are highly drawn to human energies. If you have a group that is combining their energies just think what a ghost magnet that would be!

I know the want is there. It's human nature to be curious about the unknown. But, these types of activities can cause harm and bring things into this world that should never have been here in the first place.

Take my advice.....

DON'T EVER TRY THESE ACTIVITIES! It's not worth it!

MIRRORS

For centuries many cultures around the world have believed spirits and mirrors are intertwined. Some people use them to scry to predict the future. Others believe souls travel trough them between this world and the other side. In the 1800's it was customary to cover every mirror in the house after a death, to prevent the soul from becoming trapped within them. Many people believe round mirrors are open portals that bring bad luck and negative energies into the home. Spirits have been known to appear in mirrors. Particularly, if they are antique.

If your house contains an abundant amount of mirrors it could be causing some of the activity in your home. I would suggest removing some of the mirrors from the walls and packing them away or selling them all together.

Cleanse the remaining ones with a combination of water, vinegar, and small amount of lemon juice. If you want to do a complete purification, take the mirrors outside, wipe them down with a soft cloth, and let the sun shine on them for at least 3 hours. This will pull any negative energy that may be trapped within the looking glass. After the cleansing and recharging of the mirrors your house should feel calmer and lighter.

If the mirrors were the true cause of some of the paranormal happenings, you should see the activity diminish over time.

When you purchase an antique or used mirror, be sure to purify it in the sun as stated above, before you bring it into your house. This will prevent any unwanted energies that may be trapped within it from being released into your home.

CAPTURING YOUR OWN EVIDENCE SAFELY

There are many safe ways you can capture proof of paranormal activity in your home all by yourself. I have found it is best if you are alone when you try to do this. It cuts down on any contamination of the evidence you might capture.

The first thing I would try is leaving a digital recorder on when you leave the house. Place it in the most active room. Turn it on and leave. I don't believe in asking spirits questions or provoking them to answer. This may open you up to things you really don't want around.

When you get home, return to the room and shut off the recorder. Let some time pass before you listen to it. This will give you time to relax so you won't read into every little thing you might hear on the recording.

Later that night, when it is very quiet carefully listen for anything that is out of the ordinary on the recording. Make sure you rule out anything that is of this world. Like your cat meowing in another room or a car passing on a distant road. Remember these devices are very sensitive!

If you do capture a strange sound, listen to it several times. Try to make out what it is or what the voice might be saying. Write it down and mark the time on the recording. That way you can go back and listen to it again without having to hear the whole thing every time. Try this technique several times. See if you get the same noises or voices again in the same room. Try moving it around your house. You may be surprised what goes on when you're not at home!

The next way to capture paranormal evidence in your home is with a digital camera. I have captured many paranormal anomalies in my house. I have even caught full body apparitions! It doesn't have to be a really expansive "fancy pantsy" camera, with all the bells and whistles. I just use a cheap digital camera I bought at the local department store.

There really is no secret to capturing ghosts on camera. All you need is a haunted location, a digital camera, a computer that has a zoom feature on the photo program, and patience.

My technique is very simple. I set my camera on:

Auto Scene

Super Fine Image Quality

Vivid Color

Sharp Image

High Resolution

Flash Always On

Then, I point and shoot, making sure I take at least three to five pictures in a row of the same space. Back to back pictures are the true secret. It lets you see if anything has changed in the image over time. After I have taken all the pictures I can. I upload them to my computer.

Now is where the patience comes in. One by one, slowly, looking at every inch of each picture, you may find an abnormality. If you do spot something out of the ordinary, zoom in on it and look at it more closely. Don't automatically think it is of paranormal nature. Study it and see if there is any worldly explanation first. It could be a bug or a shadow of something in the room.

The key is to know the space you are photographing so you can really see if there is something strange in your pictures.

The most important thing is...Don't ever give up! I have taken thousands of pictures over the years. Maybe one out of a hundred might have a paranormal anomaly in it. Just keep snapping pics, be patient, and maybe, just maybe, you will capture a phantom photo too!

The worst thing that can happen is, you can become obsessed with trying to capture paranormal activity. This can also open you up to things you may not want in your life. Any type of spirit interaction can open doors to unexplainable things. Some may be good and some bad, but you won't know that until it's too late. It can also interfere with daily activities. If you feel like this is becoming a problem. The best thing to do is give it a break for awhile.

I have found the more you try to capture something, that something will never show. Think of it this way: How would you like it if someone was always trying to take a picture of you or record your voice constantly? I wouldn't, and I would do my best to avoid the camera and recorder at all costs. It is the same way with spirits. Just try taking pictures and capturing recordings a few times a month. I have found the best times are during a full moon, during a thunderstorm, or when you feel like the energies in your home are high, Have fun with it, but don't let it run your life.

* If you would like to see some of my "Phantom Photos" I have captured in and around my house. You can visit my facebook page.

www.facebook.com/GhostsOfTheOldStoneHouse

Be sure to post and tell me what you think! Also feel free to like the page so you can get updates of the happenings in THE OLD STONE HOUSE.

YOU ARE NOT CRAZY

From experiences in my own life, I understand the feelings of thinking you are losing your mind! You're not going bonkers, and don't ever let anyone tell you that you are!

Doctors will say you are delusional and try to put you on antidepressants and other mind altering drugs. Yes, some people do need these types of medications for serious medical conditions. But, just because you are seeing and hearing ghosts in your house does not mean you need to be medicated. It is something that really happens!

Most people don't believe what I tell them, and I have grown very use to this. At this point in my life I don't really care what people think about me, or my gifts. I have learned to let them believe what they choose to believe. I don't argue about it anymore. It's not worth my time and effort! I know what I have witnessed and I genuinely stand by it! Plus, I have solid proof through my photography!

YOU ARE NOT CRAZY! You are privileged and gifted! Learning to manage your gifts and the paranormal activity in your home is the best thing you can do for yourself and your family. Hopefully, the information you have learned while reading this book has helped you understand your situation. How to take control of it, and maybe, just maybe, you have learned a little more about yourself!

So, the next time someone tells you are crazy when you talk about ghosts... Look at them dead in their eyes; give them a huge grin, knowing in your heart, they are the crazy one for not believing!

A MESSAGE TO MY READERS

My goal when I wrote this book was to make paranormal activity more understandable for the average person. I also hoped to show people, that just because you are living with spirits; it doesn't have to be a negative experience. It is now up to you to take charge of your home. Use the techniques I have shown you to calm your environment, and learn to live with your ghosts. Sometimes it may be challenging. As they realize you are the one in charge, the activity in your home should start to quiet down. I'm not saying it will stop all together.

Remember, they were once human beings too, and they sometimes want a little attention. Don't be afraid to say hello when you come home, or tell them you will be back later when you leave the house. I do it all the time. I have lived amicably with my ghosts for almost 15 years now. Sometimes the activity is off the charts, and at other times, it is eerily quiet. I always know they are there and I like it that way. To be honest, I think they like us too.

If you have any questions about the book, need someone to talk to who understands what you are going through, while living in a haunted house. Want to share your story, or need any help understanding what may be happening in your house. I am only an e -mail away! Please feel free to contact me anytime. I will get back to you as soon as I can. I will always be here for my readers!

My web address is:

oldstonehouseghosts@yahoo.com

I want to let all of you know, that without you, this book would just be thousands of words stored in my laptop. Thank you for taking it off the shelf and opening your hearts and minds to the paranormal. Hopefully, you have learned more about your haunted situation and how to manage it. The most important thing is, I hope you have learned a little bit more about yourself, and that you are feeling more confident about the paranormal world around you then you did before.

My wish is to hear from all of you very soon!

Blessed Be!!

Rebecca June Williford

About The Author

Rebecca June Williford was born with "sensitive gifts", in Harrisonburg, Virginia. She graduated from Harrisonburg High School in 1987, and then moved to the Richmond, Virginia area with her daughter, in 1988. She was a single mother who worked as a Nail Tech and Professional Bartender to support herself and her daughter. Rebecca married in February 2000. Soon after, the Williford family welcomed a son. The new family moved to East Tennessee in the fall of 2000. She was blessed in 2008 with her first grand daughter. Rebecca has witnessed paranormal activity since she was a child. She accepts it and understands why it occurs. She studies and follows the path of the Wiccan Faith. The Williford family still live peacefully with The Ghosts of the Old Stone House, In the beautiful mountains of East Tennessee.

Other Titles By

Rebecca June Williford

The Ghosts of the Old Stone House:

Personal Accounts of a Haunting in
East Tennessee

Living With Ghosts:

Understanding and Managing

Paranormal Activity Within Your
Home

Peculiar Paranormal Poems

Made in the USA
Lexington, KY
18 September 2014